TO

FROM

DATE

THROUGH THE BIBLE ONE RHYME AT A TIME

JIM & ELIZABETH GEORGE

·····•·•·•·•· ILLUSTRATED BY ·•·•·•·•····

SETH HAHNE

HARVEST HOUSE PUBLISHERS
EUGENE, OREGON

HARVEST KIDS is a registered trademark of The Hawkins Children's LLC. Harvest House Publishers, Inc., is the exclusive licensee of the federally registered trademark HARVEST KIDS.

Through the **Bible** one **Rhyme** at a time

Copyright © 2017 by Jim and Elizabeth George

Artwork © 2017 by Seth Hahne

Published by Harvest House Publishers

Eugene, Oregon 97402

www.harvesthousepublishers.com

Cover design by Left Coast Design

ISBN 978-0-7369-2748-2 (hardcover)

ISBN 978-0-7369-4255-3 (eBook)

Library of Congress Cataloging-in-Publication Data

Names: George, Jim, 1943-, author. || Hahne, Seth Timothy, illustrator.

Title: Through the Bible one rhyme at a time / Jim and Elizabeth George; artwork by Seth Hahne.

Description: Eugene, Oregon: Harvest House Publishers, 2017. || Description based on print version record and CIP data provided by publisher; resource not viewed.

Subjects: LCSH: Bible stories, English. || Children's poetry, American.

Classification: LCC BS559 (ebook) || LCC BS559 .G46 2017 (print) || DDC 22095/05—dc23

LC record available at https://lccn.loc.gov/2016057820

Printed in China

17 18 19 20 21 22 23 24 25 / **IM** / 10 9 8 7 6 5 4 3 2 1

Dear friend,

There is nothing quite as special as the young ones in your life! And nothing is as rewarding as helping those young minds understand God's message of love and instruction for living His way.

You have a tremendous opportunity to expose your precious little ones to God's Word and His truths by using your own voice and pictures that illustrate these truths in a way that helps kids grasp God's story. This brilliantly illustrated and fun rhyme Bible was created for you and the young ones you are nurturing in God's ways. From Genesis to Revelation, this children's Bible will teach little ones the flow of the Bible—one rhyme at a time. You will even find a prayer for your little ones to pray at the end of each page, a prayer that will help seal God's wisdom and knowledge into their hearts.

So gather up your little ones and come along! Introduce them to the unchanging Scriptures, which teach them the right things to do and the right choices to make. Let them see how God's way is always the best way! You'll be delighted as you witness the seeds you are planting into precious little hearts begin to bear fruit. Lead them through the Bible...one rhyme at a time.

In His everlasting love,

Jim and Elizabeth George

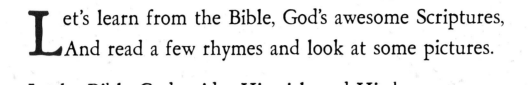

L et's learn from the Bible, God's awesome Scriptures,
And read a few rhymes and look at some pictures.

In the Bible God guides His girls and His boys
To do what He says and make the right choice.

4

In Bible adventures the heroes are brave.
    You, too, can trust God and not be afraid.

You'll see how God loves you as we read each line,
    And learn from His story—one rhyme at a time.

In the beginning, where God starts His story,
We find His creation, which shows us His glory.

God's best creation was Adam and Eve,
Who lived in His garden...till they were deceived.

"What have you done?" God asked His new couple.
"We disobeyed You. Now we're in big trouble!"

When man grew more sinful, God knew it was time
To destroy what was evil and punish all crime.

To Noah God came and said, "I'm charging you—
Build an ark, get your family, all beasts two by two.

"Rain, death, and chaos are coming to earth
So man can start over with a brand-new birth!"

When the sun came out, God gave a bright sign—
A rainbow to promise that all would be fine.

*Thank You, dear God, for mankind's fresh start
So now I can love You with all of my heart.*

When Noah's clan grew to fill all creation,
God chose Abraham to start a new nation.

He waited a l-o-n-g time for a child in his life,
Then God gave him Isaac through Sarah, his wife.

Isaac, their son, and Rebekah, his wife,
Had twin boys who caused nothing but strife.

Dad doted on Esau—Mom loved Jacob, his brother.
(Too bad they were naughty and hated each other!)

Jacob was tricky and deceived his big brother,
Then ran in fear to the clan of his mother.

Twelve sons were born during Jacob's new life,
But he favored young Joseph, causing great strife.

Jealous brothers sold Joseph and took his bright coat—
He was taken to Egypt, a slave without hope.

I see now my family should all love each other,
And that includes loving my sister and brother!

G od helped Joseph to know what was right
To understand dreams with awesome insight.

Joseph told Pharaoh what his dream was about:
"Seven years of food—and seven years without."

With plenty of food and Joseph in charge,
He brought his kin to Egypt to live and enlarge.

They became slaves, yet grew stronger each year.
"Kill the boy babies!" Pharaoh said out of fear.

Wee baby Moses was hidden with care
In a basket on the river—who would look there?

But Pharaoh's own daughter found Moses inside!
He was a prince—till he fled to hide.

You watch over Your people, though near or far,
Moses, Joseph—and me!—wherever we are.

Moses heard God's voice, while walking about,
Say from a bush: "Lead My people out!"

God demanded of Pharaoh, "Let My people go!"
He sent ten plagues on Egypt, His power to show.

While the water turned red and bugs filled the air,
All of God's people were safe in His care.

When they finally left Egypt, with God by their side,
God gave Ten Commandments to act as their guide.

God promised them a land where they could stay,
But ten spies saw giants, and they ran away!

Caleb and Joshua said, "Don't be afraid,
The God of our fathers will come to our aid."

Because no one listened, they wandered years in the sand,
Till a new generation would take the Promised Land.

Lord, when I'm scared, help me to know
You're by my side, wherever I go.

Because Moses could not go into the Promised Land,
God chose the warrior Joshua to be in command.

Joshua fought battles, as God told him to do,
   Till the land and its people were finally subdued.

When Joshua died, judges ruled in his place,
   Directing the nation in the trials they faced.

With a plan in hand, a war was begun.
   Using Deborah and Barak, God's people won!

The foes numbered in thousands, Gideon had 300 men,
   With pots, horns—and a shout!—they won in the end.

Samson—the strongest of Israel's men—
   Battled the Philistines again and again.

Ruth loved the true God of heaven and earth
   And joined Jesus' line through her little son's birth.

You cared for others every step of the way!
Thank You for caring for me every day.

Childless Hannah prayed to God for a son.
God gave her Samuel, a most godly one.

Samuel, God's prophet, led and taught with great fame.
Other nations had kings. Israel wanted the same.

Saul became king to the people's delight,
But he strayed from God—his heart wasn't right.

Young David, a shepherd, cared for flocks as they grazed,
Fought lions and bears, sang to God with great praise.

Defeating Goliath with a stone and a sling,
David loved God and was later crowned king!

The warrior-king David made the nation quite grand.
He reigned in Jerusalem where God's temple would stand.

David longed to build God a place that was great!
But God said, "Not now. My temple can wait."

Make me like these heroes who followed You.
They trusted God—that's what I want too!

David's son, Solomon, was given great wisdom,
Building God's temple and expanding his kingdom.

When Solomon sinned, God split the kingdom in two.
There was north, there was south. False worship grew.

Up north, Israel's kings were bad from the start.
Down south, Judah's kings sometimes had a good heart.

Elijah used miracles to deal with great sin,
And rode on a chariot to heaven in the end!

Elisha did miracles, and the people were fed.
He even raised one little boy from the dead!

God sent more prophets just like these two men,
But the people rebelled again and again.

God's chosen people wouldn't keep His commands,
So He sent them away from their
Promised Land.

I need Your wisdom to know right from wrong,
To choose what is right, to stand up and be strong.

God's prophets told people what they heard and saw.
He showed them the future—they marveled in awe.

The four Major Prophets began as young men.
  They preached to the people again and again.

The prophet Isaiah had a great message to tell...
  "A Savior is coming—named Immanuel!"

Next Jeremiah came preaching with tears:
  "Turn back to God—don't be punished for years!"

Because Daniel prayed, he was thrown in a lions' den
  Where God kept him safe and brought him out again.

God spoke to Daniel through visions and dreams
  And showed him a future that no one had seen.

Help me, like Your prophets, to hear what You say
And share the good news of what's coming someday.

Twelve Minor Prophets are next in order.
They're just as important but quite a bit shorter.

Jonah was one. God called him to preach
To a nation that Jonah thought couldn't be reached.

Instead of obeying what God had to say,
He jumped on a ship and sailed away.

God sent a storm...the boat started sinking.
"It's my fault," said Jonah. "What was I thinking!

"Throw me in the water, and this storm will end."
As soon as they did, it was sunny again.

A giant fish swallowed him right then and there.
For three days the prophet cried out in prayer.

God forgave Jonah—he was relieved!
He preached to the people, and they all believed!

Dear Lord, when You give me something to do,
Help me to always say yes to You.

The Persian King Cyrus sent out a decree:
"No longer captives, the Jews are now free!"

One group returned with a task that was simple:
"Go to Jerusalem and rebuild the temple."

Rebuilding God's temple ended at last,
Then Ezra the priest taught the Law from the past.

Nehemiah, a servant, heard of Jerusalem's sad plight:
The walls were all down and must be made right.

He marched to Jerusalem and faced opposition,
But the walls were rebuilt—he finished his mission!

In Persia, a new queen would need to be found.
The Jewish girl Esther was chosen and crowned.

"Murder the Jews!" was the villain's bold plea,
But God saved them all—through Esther's bravery.

I really like those who were faithful and true.
Make me like them—to be used by You too!

The Bible has two parts, both full of God's glory,
Old and New Testaments—but just one story!

When Mary hears from an angel, the "new" part begins:
"Behold, you'll have a Son whose reign never ends."

God spoke to Joseph one night in a dream,
"It's okay to wed Mary. Things aren't what they seem."

Joseph did what God said and took Mary, his bride,
To list their names in Bethlehem for a census worldwide.

When told no rooms in the inn were available,
Mary birthed Jesus in the animals' stable!

Shepherds found Jesus that very same night,
While angels praised God and the heavens shone bright.

"We want to see Jesus!" Wise men came from afar,
Bringing gifts to the babe after following His star.

Lord, You sent Jesus to save me from sin.
Thank You for loving me and for sending Him.

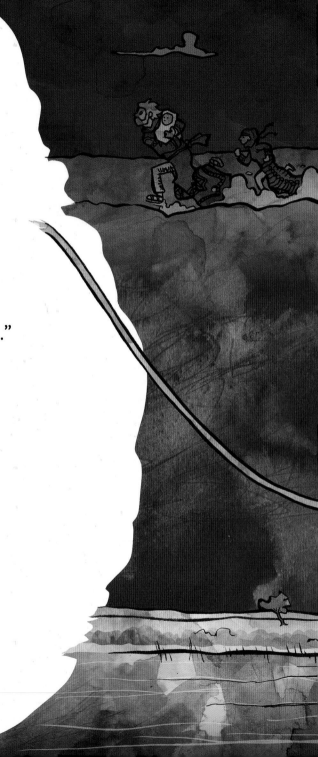

Joseph and Mary presented Jesus, their boy
To fulfill God's Law and express their great joy.

Herod was angry when he heard the news.
He didn't want Jesus to be king of the Jews.

God said to Joseph, "To Egypt! Go hide!"
There Jesus stayed until King Herod died.

At twelve, Jesus stayed at the Temple to worship,
Saying, "Mom, I must be where my Father's work is."

When Jesus was grown, He went looking for John,
Who was preaching and baptizing all the day long.

John baptized Jesus as God's special One.
God said from heaven, "I'm pleased with My Son."

Jesus was tempted by Satan—40 days!
But Jesus said, "No. I follow God's ways."

I'm grateful for family and the home where I stay.
Help me live like You by following God's way.

Peter and John fished each day on the sea,
But Jesus called, "Come fish for men—follow Me!"

Jesus told Matthew, "You too—follow Me!"
And Matthew invited his friends to come see.

Jesus prayed through the night and chose twelve men
To tell the whole world of God's love for them.

Nicodemus, a teacher, found Jesus and then
Jesus told him, "You must be born again."

A woman met Jesus beside a deep well.
He gave her living water—and a message to tell.

He told of God's kingdom and who would take part:
The meek and the kind and the pure in heart.

He spoke parables to those who would hear.
They loved His stories that made God's truth clear.

You show me Your wonderful love and Your care.
Help me be more like You—that is my prayer.

At a wedding in Cana, as guests sat to dine,
Jesus turned everyday water to wine!

A father asked Jesus, "Please come heal my son."
    "Go," Jesus said, "and it will be done."

Ten lepers shouted, "Have mercy today!"
    And Jesus healed them as they went away.

A little girl died and was laid on her bed.
    But when Jesus touched her, she got up instead.

A huge crowd with Jesus had nothing for lunch.
    With a few loaves and fish, Jesus fed the whole
bunch!

He walked on water as if it were land.
    Peter tried too but needed a hand.

When those in the boat saw what Jesus had done,
    They worshipped Him, saying, "You are God's Son."

Seeing the wonderful things that You do,
I know that You will take care of me too.

Jesus then knew it was time for good-bye:
To Jerusalem He went—to suffer and die.

He arrived on a donkey while the multitude roared,
"Bless Him who comes in the name of the Lord!"

At His last supper, the disciples gathered to eat,
While Jesus took a towel and washed their feet.

Jesus prayed to His Father after dinner was done:
To Gethsemane they went, for His hour had come.

With tears Jesus knelt in the garden to pray,
Asking God's help to do His will the next day.

Judas showed up with some guards and a plan:
"The one that I kiss—he is your man!"

Jesus was innocent, as Pilate well knew,
Yet the sentence of death he refused to undo.

You chose to die! It's hard to understand,
But I'm glad that You love me as part of God's plan.

A crown of sharp thorns, soldiers made Jesus wear.
They beat Him and mocked Him—it just wasn't fair.

Nailed to the cross with not long to live,
Still Jesus prayed, "Father, forgive."

He said, "It's finished!" and in a tomb was laid:
By His death, the price for mankind's sin was paid.

The tomb soon was empty as Jesus had said.
An angel announced, "He's risen from the dead!"

Mary Magdalene was first to arrive.
Jesus said, "Go tell My friends I'm alive!"

Thomas said, "No—it's too good to be true."
But when He saw Jesus, he believed too!

Jesus has told us what we are to do:
"Go make disciples, and I'll be with you!"

I'm sorry for all of the pain You went through,
But thank You for dying so I can know You.

Jesus told many after He rose from the dead,
"I'm alive! Don't worry! There's nothing to dread."

When Jesus' time here on earth was all done,
He said, "Now you finish the work I've begun."

Sounding like wind and looking like flame,
The Holy Spirit helped many preach in God's name.

A lame man was told, "In Jesus' name, walk!"
He leaped up and praised God—that made people talk!

When Peter explained, "That is Jesus' power,"
Thousands and thousands believed in that hour!

The new church was growing; the people were living
A new life of loving and sharing and giving.

God said to Peter, "The time has now come
To tell the whole world—I love everyone!"

Because You're alive and with me right here,
I can feel safe—I have nothing to fear.

The news of Jesus spread through Jerusalem town,
And evil Saul began to hunt the Christians down.

To Damascus the Christians began to run and flee,
Till Jesus asked Saul, "Why do you persecute Me?"

Saul was blinded by God till a man touched his eyes,
Then Saul followed Jesus, like those he'd despised.

Because he preached Jesus, the Jews tried to kill Saul,
But friends helped him escape up and over a wall!

Those in Jerusalem judged Saul unworthy of trust.
His faith couldn't be real—"Look how he treated us!"

Barnabas spoke up, describing Saul's new zeal,
His encounter with Christ, why Saul's faith was real.

The Spirit chose these two men to be God's team,
To witness and preach, His people to redeem.

I like how Saul changed when he believed in You.
I want to have "real faith" to share with others too.

A group left Antioch and were led by Saul,
And somehow, along the way, "Saul" became "Paul."

Paul took three trips to preach of God's grace,
Setting up churches in each port and place.

Held in jail to die for his preaching and zeal,
As a Roman, Paul demanded, "To Caesar I appeal!"

The people on Malta cared for Paul in their home
When his ship wrecked while sailing to Caesar in Rome.

After three months of waiting—and being bitten by a snake!—
He again sailed for Rome, his petition to make.

In Rome, Paul wrote and taught of God's grace
While waiting for Caesar to hear his case.

Paul wrote 13 letters describing Jesus' power,
Saying, "He's coming again, arriving at any hour!"

I'm glad You protected Paul all along the way,
So I can read his letters in my Bible every day!

In the book of Hebrews, here's what you'll read:
Christ is "better than" anything. He's all that you need.

There's one verse in Hebrews that says of God's Word,
It's alive and it's active, sharper than any sword!

James, brother of Jesus, wrote about real faith—
"Faith with good works" must be lived out each day.

Peter wrote to Christians who were so far away,
"Suffer with joy—Jesus will be back one day."

John, Jesus' close friend, wrote three little letters:
"Love one another. Stand for truth. Correct errors."

Jude, kin to Jesus, said, "Christians, be wise!
Beware of false teachers! Don't fall for their lies!"

John saw a vision of things that will take place.
The big ending is next—the story of God's grace.

Revelation tells people about God's future plan.
It reveals what He says will happen to man.

Jesus comes again in this wonderful story,
Riding a white horse with angels in glory.

He came once as a servant, salvation to bring.
This time He'll come as a conquering king!

He'll bind up the devil—as His great first task—
He'll rule with His saints, a thousand years to last.

Judging all people from His white throne is next,
Checking their names with the Book of Life's text.

From heaven above, new Jerusalem descends,
Full of God's glory—a blazing light without end,

Where God and His Son, on their glorious throne,
Are forever loving and ruling their own.

Jesus, help me to walk with You every day
Till we are together in heaven to stay.

FIND IT IN THE BIBLE